WHEELS OF LIFE

**Copyright © 2017
by Sandeep Ravidutt Sharma**

All rights reserved. No part of this book may be reproduced or transmitted in any form or by any means without written permission from the author.

If you have further questions, contact on

Phone: +919969256731
Email: sandeepraviduttsharma@gmail.com

Cover Designed By:
Bhagyashri Sharma

Dedication

This book is dedicated to **Shani Dev**, the Lord of Justice. He is endowed with a divine mission of punishing bad deeds and reward good ones. He presides over righteousness and unrighteousness in the world. Shani Dev maintains the precarious balance between good and evil in this world. None can escape the effects of their doings as he presides over our Karma.

To please **Lord Shani**, praying for the success of my readers in social, political, traditional, spiritual, career, educational and business areas, i hereby recite the following mantra...

"Om Praam Prim Prom Sah Shanaye Namaha"

© **WHEELS OF LIFE**
BY SANDEEP RAVIDUTT SHARMA

Table of Contents

Foreword I
Wheels of Life...1

© **WHEELS OF LIFE**
BY SANDEEP RAVIDUTT SHARMA

Foreword

This book provides you with a list of 100 positive, inspiring and motivating quotes churned out by my mind with the grace of almighty God. I'm sure if you keep reading and referring to these thoughts and quotes, you will draw inspiration and *Wheels of Life* would surely move towards *success* and *happiness*. This book is just a small attempt by me, inspired by Shani Dev, to always follow the path of righteousness and remember that no one can escape from the effects of their doings. Justice will be done at all cost. When the time comes, he weighs the good and bad deeds of living beings and accordingly rewards or bestow punishment and purifies the Soul.

"Those who follow the path of TRUTH and embrace positivity never gets lost in the jungle of ignorance and darkness."

I sincerely hope, you will find this book amazing, interesting, rejuvenating, unique and a constant source of Inspiration.

Thank You and Happy Reading.

© **WHEELS OF LIFE**
BY SANDEEP RAVIDUTT SHARMA

Walking on the righteous path carrying the flag of TRUTH needs courage.

© **WHEELS OF LIFE**
BY SANDEEP RAVIDUTT SHARMA

Accept your faults in time and you can still rebuild your relationship.

© **WHEELS OF LIFE**
BY SANDEEP RAVIDUTT SHARMA

Pursue your IDEAS to convert them into reality.

© **WHEELS OF LIFE**
BY SANDEEP RAVIDUTT SHARMA

Winner always finishes in time.

© **WHEELS OF LIFE**
BY SANDEEP RAVIDUTT SHARMA

Assumptions often leads to wrong judgement. Don't assume.

© WHEELS OF LIFE
BY SANDEEP RAVIDUTT SHARMA

Avoid quick decision if you are not satisfied or doubt the outcome of the proposed activity. Decide quickly when it's matter of life and death.

© WHEELS OF LIFE
BY SANDEEP RAVIDUTT SHARMA

Caring for each other makes the journey of life interesting.

© **WHEELS OF LIFE**
BY SANDEEP RAVIDUTT SHARMA

Celebrate each moment instead of making plans for a grand Celebration.

© **WHEELS OF LIFE**
BY SANDEEP RAVIDUTT SHARMA

Dark clouds introduce rains to the world with a thunder. Rains provide breath of life. Love dark clouds and rains alike.

© **WHEELS OF LIFE**
BY SANDEEP RAVIDUTT SHARMA

Commit to your own self before you commit to the world.

© **WHEELS OF LIFE**
BY SANDEEP RAVIDUTT SHARMA

Curiosity makes you learn and gain in life.

Don't become slave of your DESIRE, instead become MASTER of your actions.

© WHEELS OF LIFE
BY SANDEEP RAVIDUTT SHARMA

Don't beg unless there is no way to save someone's life.

© WHEELS OF LIFE
BY SANDEEP RAVIDUTT SHARMA

Don't blame others when you lose. Own your debacle and make attempt to rise as a winner.

© **WHEELS OF LIFE**
BY SANDEEP RAVIDUTT SHARMA

Don't expect Apple if you have planted Cactus.

© **WHEELS OF LIFE**
BY SANDEEP RAVIDUTT SHARMA

Don't lose your identity by trying to please everyone.

Don't trade happiness for money. Anyways you can't trade money for happiness.

© **WHEELS OF LIFE**
BY SANDEEP RAVIDUTT SHARMA

*Don't treat
'Commitment' just like
any another word. It
reflects your character
and showcases your
TRUSTWORTHINESS.*

Ego centric behaviour makes us lose real friends who actually cared. Shed your eGO.

© WHEELS OF LIFE
BY SANDEEP RAVIDUTT SHARMA

Enjoy the FREEDOM responsibly.

© WHEELS OF LIFE
BY SANDEEP RAVIDUTT SHARMA

Even when you don't know where to go.... KEEP GOING. You will find purpose of your life.

© WHEELS OF LIFE
BY SANDEEP RAVIDUTT SHARMA

Everyone wants to grow in life but only few really make efforts to achieve greater heights.

Expectation is the root cause of unhappiness. Focus on efforts and not expectations.

© **WHEELS OF LIFE**
BY SANDEEP RAVIDUTT SHARMA

Experience always help you the next time. It's your efforts and positive attitude that helps you to win today.

Feel the world full of happiness. Fill the world with kindness. Kindness makes everyone HAPPY.

© **WHEELS OF LIFE**
BY SANDEEP RAVIDUTT SHARMA

Finishing last in a competition is thousand times better than QUITTING.

Great achievers would never lie to achieve.

© **WHEELS OF LIFE**
BY SANDEEP RAVIDUTT SHARMA

Great day begins today.

Great works are laid on strong foundation of knowledge, determination and efforts. Accidental accomplishment cannot be termed as Great works.

Happiness is similar to raining flowers in your life. Flowers are both pretty and smells good. Be happy.

Harsh words destroy the bridge of friendship. Choose words to encourage and not discourage.

© **WHEELS OF LIFE**
BY SANDEEP RAVIDUTT SHARMA

Hope never dies whether you win or lose.

© **WHEELS OF LIFE**
BY SANDEEP RAVIDUTT SHARMA

Hope returns to Earth every morning with the Sun rise.

© **WHEELS OF LIFE**
BY SANDEEP RAVIDUTT SHARMA

Hopes are afloat for those who intend to reach their destination.

If you could not save human life, atleast console and support those who are left behind.

© **WHEELS OF LIFE**
BY SANDEEP RAVIDUTT SHARMA

Innocence cannot be taught. Never let innocence die.

It's not that important what you achieved in life, but how your journey was.

© WHEELS OF LIFE
BY SANDEEP RAVIDUTT SHARMA

It's preferable to be tagged NOBODY rather than somebody who is cruel, rude and inhuman.

© **WHEELS OF LIFE**
BY SANDEEP RAVIDUTT SHARMA

Just to maximise your returns don't forget humanity.

© **WHEELS OF LIFE**
BY SANDEEP RAVIDUTT SHARMA

Lead your desire in place of being led by it.

© **WHEELS OF LIFE**
BY SANDEEP RAVIDUTT SHARMA

Life comes in limited edition format. Make the most out of it. Don't waste it in useless arguments, sort all your issues amicably.

© **WHEELS OF LIFE**
BY SANDEEP RAVIDUTT SHARMA

Life doesn't give you undo option.

Life gives a red carpet welcome to those who never shied away to lay the rug before they deserved to walk on the same.

© **WHEELS OF LIFE**
BY SANDEEP RAVIDUTT SHARMA

Live and Let Live is one of the best policy which promotes harmony and universal development.

© **WHEELS OF LIFE**
BY SANDEEP RAVIDUTT SHARMA

Live NOW. Tomorrow is just an illusion.

Mistakes committed makes you richer in experience.

Moon never gives up its ongoing crusade against dark forces. Even when it gets decimated Moon doesn't quit, it rises again to thwart the dark forces. When Moon can do it every night. Why can't we?

© WHEELS OF LIFE
BY SANDEEP RAVIDUTT SHARMA

Nature branches out in all direction to greet you. Embrace nature with gratitude and be part of it.

Never lie to anyone especially to those who trust you.

© **WHEELS OF LIFE**
BY SANDEEP RAVIDUTT SHARMA

Never mind someone's harsh words when you are aware of the current turbulence in that person's life. Do your best to rescue such souls in time.

© **WHEELS OF LIFE**
BY SANDEEP RAVIDUTT SHARMA

Never misunderstand someone unless you have heard his/her side of the story. Sometimes what you see is half the truth. Take a 360 degree view and then decide what is right or wrong. Don't try to explain someone who always wears an ear plug. Explore and truth reveals itself sooner or later.

Nobody can accompany you till the end. Even your own shadow leaves you after covering certain distance or time. Be prepared to fight your life battle all alone.

© **WHEELS OF LIFE**
BY SANDEEP RAVIDUTT SHARMA

Pearls of wisdom demands your patience and effort.

People are not furniture who can be chosen and placed in a room. Sentiments, emotions and thoughts reside deep within each of us. Respect these sentiments and expressions.

People around you may inspire without them being aware of it. Draw inspiration from whatever source and KEEP GOING.

© WHEELS OF LIFE
BY SANDEEP RAVIDUTT SHARMA

People don't stop living near the Sea just for the fear of Tsunami. Same way, don't just stop TRYING due to the fear of failure.

Positive energy doesn't need any introduction. You can feel it instantly.

Positivity rules your action and influences your achievement.

© **WHEELS OF LIFE**
BY SANDEEP RAVIDUTT SHARMA

Possibilities are unlimited for those who have understood their own limitations.

Possibilities are unlimited. All you have to do is focus on the subject matter with an uncluttered mind. Start your day with a bang....It's your day today....and you are here to win....

Rains don't discriminate between rich and poor. Always share good things in life without any discrimination.

© **WHEELS OF LIFE**
BY SANDEEP RAVIDUTT SHARMA

Real test of your CHARACTER happens during period of distress.

Remember it's the rain drops that ultimately makes an Ocean. Together we can win.

Shed your eGo and attribute all kinds of deed to the almighty. Dedicate all your Karma to the Lord or the creator.

© **WHEELS OF LIFE**
BY SANDEEP RAVIDUTT SHARMA

Sometimes WAR is the only option left to restore peace. But at all times PEACE is the only way a war can end.

Sometimes what you see is not the complete truth. Truth is eternal and is revealed at the right time...

Stay positive by ignoring negative beings who only knows to paint black.

© WHEELS OF LIFE
BY SANDEEP RAVIDUTT SHARMA

Sun is quite clear about its mission. It retires every evening and gives chance to Moon and Stars to take over the task of illuminating the world. Same way, keep up your promises and let others do their role.

Sun looks amazing even when it retires for the day. Hope of billions rest on the next Sun rise.

Sun meets Sea every day for billions of years. The routine is consistently followed without any ego. Why can't we shed our eGo and meet half way and resolve our differences.

Swimming against the river flow can lead to complete burnout. Each attempt will bring you back to the starting point.

Thank God for each breath and not just for your wealth and status.

Things or people that appear impressive sometimes turn up the other way round. Impression is no doubt important, depends to some extent on your outward appearance but more on your inner strength and core values.

Think of cleaning the garbage and not just the garbage. You attract whatever you visualise.

© **WHEELS OF LIFE**
BY SANDEEP RAVIDUTT SHARMA

To begin something new, you may have to end the current one. In the bargain, be prepared to gain or lose some.

To fulfill your dreams you don't have to be a PhD. Simplicity can achieve anything complex.

To give your approval for a cause you don't have to shout. You can simply nod and the world would know.

© **WHEELS OF LIFE**
BY SANDEEP RAVIDUTT SHARMA

To succeed you may need short, medium or long term plans. But remember only action oriented plan works the best.

Truth cannot remain under the carpet for long. Truth unveils itself at the right time and all false notions are buried forever.

© WHEELS OF LIFE
BY SANDEEP RAVIDUTT SHARMA

Truth never lies

Try to change the world when you could successfully change your own self.

Try to change your attitude and imbibe positive traits. The world around you would change within minutes.

Vertical growth looks good but leads to losing ground contact. Keep growing vertically but pay regular visit to the ground and lift those who need your help to grow. This way your success will be meaningful and full of satisfaction.

© WHEELS OF LIFE
BY SANDEEP RAVIDUTT SHARMA

Walk away from a place where immorality rules. Morality strengthens your resolve to win.

Walk away from your own selfish attitude and unkind conduct. Life is beautiful.

© WHEELS OF LIFE
BY SANDEEP RAVIDUTT SHARMA

War are won by those who had self belief and clarity of the goal post.

War only ends on the surface when someone wins.

Wars mongers die a natural death when both sides are listening to each other attentively.

Whatever you do, never leave any scope to regret.

Whatever you paint on your mind with brush of your heart will be delivered by the Universe.

Wheels not attached to a vehicle are of no use. It is similar to a person having so much of knowledge and talent but who doesn't know how and where to apply. Knowledge when applied shines.

© WHEELS OF LIFE
BY SANDEEP RAVIDUTT SHARMA

Wheels on their own can't do much. It's the role of the navigator which is critical for the wheel to move. The Navigator uses this wheel, form an alignment, set the process of rolling, stirs it in the right direction. Wheels of life are none other than us. Navigator is your Guru or God.

When a door opens for you, it may offer you opportunities as well as shocks. The challenge lies in how do you tame the unknown to your advantage.

When you have the option to live and die in this world. Choose the option to live happily; understanding and supporting each other wholeheartedly.

When you inspire someone, the motivation comes back to you to inspire further.

Whether the glass is half full or half empty. You have to decide.

Whether you earn in rupee or dollar hardly matters. At the end of the day how much you could spend decides whether it was worth the effort.

Whether you notice or not but your subconscious mind notices everything.

Winner hardly thinks about the loser and gets carried away with the celebration. Those who win and still take out time to motivate the losers are the exceptional ones with a kind and human heart. Winning the game is good but winning the hearts is Gold.

© **WHEELS OF LIFE**
BY SANDEEP RAVIDUTT SHARMA

You just can't escape from the problems of the world. Why not face them head on and emerge as a WINNER.

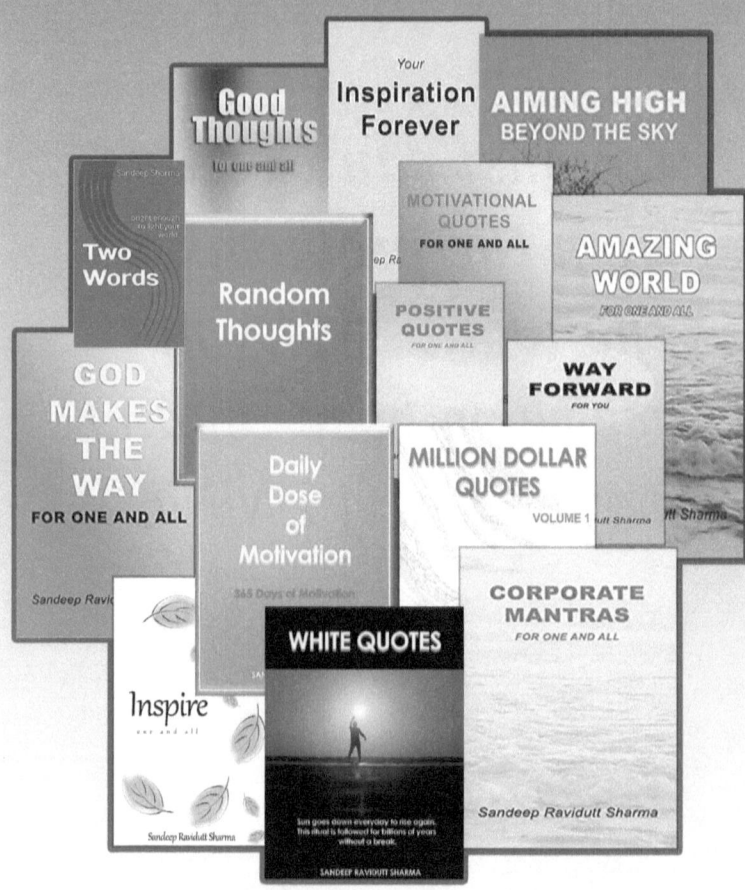

www.ingramcontent.com/pod-product-compliance
Lightning Source LLC
Chambersburg PA
CBHW031439210526
45464CB00005B/2264